The Ultimate Picnic Cookbook

Tasty Recipes for A Fun and Fuss-Free Picnic

By: Logan King

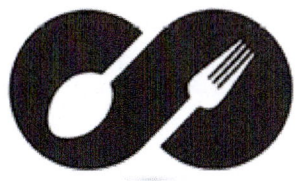

Copyright © 2021 by Logan King

Edition Notice

The author has taken any step to make sure this book is accurate and safe. Every info is checked. However, every step you take following the book do it with caution and on your own accord.

If you end up with a copied and illegal version of this book please delete it and get the original. This will support the author to create even better books for everyone. Also, if possible report where you have found the illegal version.

This book is under copyright license which means no one is allowed to make any changes, prints, copies, republish or sell it except for the author.

Table of Contents

Introduction 6

Recipes 9

    Sunset Rice 10

    Watermelon Ice Lollies 13

    Salad In a Cup 1 15

    Salad In a Cup 2 17

    Salad In a Cup 3 19

    Melon and Strawberry Fruit Salad 21

    Fancy Fruit and Cheese Cups 23

    Virgin Mimosa 25

    Turkey Croissant Sandwiches 27

    Sweet Kebabs 29

    Caprese Salad in A Cup 31

    Rainbow In a Cup 33

    Cucumber Sandwiches 35

    Easy Peasy Chocolate Cornflake Cups 37

Rice Krispies Squares 39

Savory Snack Box 41

Fruit Snack Box 43

Salted Caramel Popcorn 45

Cheesy Popcorn 47

Avocado and Chickpea Sandwiches 49

Snack Box 51

Spinach and Mushroom Frittata 53

Butter Herb Corn 55

Lemon Coconut Squares 57

Peanut Butter and Jelly Sandwiches 59

Turkey Sandwiches 61

Sandwich and Fruit Kebab 63

Tuna and Avocado Wrap 65

Easy Picnic Brownies 67

Banana and Peanut Butter Rice Cakes 70

Conclusion 72

About the Author 73

Appendices 74

Introduction

Top 5 tips for a perfect picnic: These tips will help you make the perfect picnic for you, your family and friends to enjoy.

1. **Choose The Right Location**

A great picnic is all about the location. Choosing a wonderful location can add to the ambience of the picnic and even encourage you to spend more time enjoying the company of people you are with. You need to look for somewhere that has beautiful scenery, grassy and lush to make it comfortable to sit. Make sure there is plenty of natural shade, for example, under a tree. It is also good to make sure there is a lot of space around for children to play and for privacy. If it happens to rain on your picnic day, don't worry. You can always set up your picnic indoors.

2. **Pack Right**

COOLER: When you look online, the most common picnic food carrier you will see is a wicker basket. Baskets are good if you're only packing food that should be kept at room temperature. However, if you are packing food that should be kept warm or cold, it is best to use an insulated cooler.

BLANKET: Blankets are an essential part of a picnic, but they don't have to be an actual blanket. You can use a plastic mat for easy clean up or a small cotton sheet that can easily be cleaned.

PLATES/UTENSILS: Make sure that you pack the right serving materials for your food: reusable plates, knives and forks and napkins.

THROW PILLOWS: Pillows are useful because they make the picnic more comfortable and encourage more conversation with everyone.

WET WIPES/TISSUES/SANITIZER: Picnics can be very messy, so packing cleaning materials is very important.

DISPOSABLE BAGS: These are used for cleaning up and putting all the rubbish in to keep the flies away.

3. **Keep It Simple**

Great picnics are about no-fuss food. To minimize your prep time, keep the menu as simple and easy as you can.

4. **Bring Entertainment**

Picnics are all about fun, so it's a good idea to pack some entertainment. It can be outdoor friendly games like cards, Jenga, twister, etc. It's also a good idea to look up age-appropriate group activity games.

5. **Clean Up**

Common courtesy that is often forgotten is cleaning up after yourself. It is the important picnic etiquette to make sure you leave your picnic spot as clean as when you found it.

Recipes

Sunset Rice

This dish is the perfect recipe for a sunset picnic. It has vegetables that mimic the colours of sunset; red, orange and yellow. Full of simple but delicious flavour, it can be served hot, warm or even cold.

Serving Size: 4 people

Cooking Time: 20 mins

Ingredients:

- 1 cup of long-grain rice
- 1 red bell pepper (chopped)
- 1 orange bell pepper (chopped)
- 1 large carrot (grated)
- ½ (500g) can of sweetcorn (drained)
- 1 large red onion
- ½ teaspoon of salt
- ½ teaspoon of black pepper
- 1 teaspoon of paprika
- 1 teaspoon of allspice
- 1 tablespoon of oil

Method:

In a pan, cook the rice according to the instructions on its packet.

In another large pan, heat up the oil and add the onion.

Once the onion is softened, add all the spices and stir well.

Then, add the carrot, sweetcorn and bell peppers and make sure everything is mixed well together.

Once they have softened, remove from the heat.

Once the rice is cooked, remove from the heat. Add to the large pan with the vegetables and mix well.

Make sure the rice and vegetables are mixed well together and place in a warming container.

Take to the picnic and enjoy.

N.B: you can pack the rice in separate silver containers for easy distribution.

Watermelon Ice Lollies

These lollies are great for a picnic in the middle of summer. They are guaranteed to please adults and kids. A sweet surprise with a citrus twist!

Serving Size: 4-12 people (depending on the size of the watermelon)

Cooking Time: 10 mins (minimum 2 hours freezing)

Ingredients:

- 1 medium sweet watermelon
- 6 lemons (juiced)

Method:

Cut the watermelon into slices and divide each slice into 4 triangles.

Insert a popsicle stick in the rind of the watermelon triangles in the centre.

On a tray, place the watermelon triangles down.

With a toothpick, poke a few holes into the watermelon triangles evenly covering the surface.

Pour over the lemon juice making sure each watermelon triangle is covered with it.

Place the tray in the freezer for a minimum of 2 hours.

Pack your watermelon lollies in a cooling container and take to your picnic.

Salad In a Cup 1

This is a great recipe that makes serving salad easy and stress-free. The salad uses superfood spinach as its base, so it is full of great vitamins and minerals.

Serving Size: 4 people

Cooking Time: 15 mins

Ingredients:

- ½ cup of Greek yogurt (or any plain yogurt)
- ½ teaspoon of mixed herbs
- ¼ teaspoon of salt
- ½ teaspoon of black pepper
- 1 cup of cherry tomatoes (chopped)
- ¼ cup of black olives
- 2 cups of baby spinach
- 1 cup of romaine (or iceberg) lettuce (chopped)

Method:

In a large bowl, mix the yogurt, herbs, salt and pepper.

Get 4 plastic cups that have covers and divide the yogurt dressing evenly at the bottom of the cups.

Add the olives and tomatoes.

Then, top with the spinach and lettuce.

Cover the cups and place them in a cooling container.

Take to your picnic and enjoy.

Salad In a Cup 2

This is a great recipe that makes serving salad easy and stress-free. It uses sweet vegetables to help make it flavourful and colourful.

Serving Size: 4 people

Cooking Time: 15 mins

Ingredients:

- 2 large lemons
- ¼ cup of extra virgin olive oil
- 1 tablespoon of mixed herbs
- ½ teaspoon of salt
- ½ teaspoon of black pepper
- ½ iceberg lettuce (chopped)
- 1 cup of cherry tomatoes (cut in half)
- 1 green bell pepper (cut into slices)
- ½ cup of radishes (cut into thin slices)
- ½ cup of sweet corn

Method:

In a small bowl, mix together the oil, salt, pepper and mixed herbs and pour into a plastic bottle.

In a large bowl, mix all the ingredients together.

Divide the salad into 4 plastic containers and cover.

Pack the salad containers and dressing bottle into a cooler.

When you are ready to serve, pour some dressing into each containers, cover and shake well.

Salad In a Cup 3

This is a great recipe that makes serving salad easy and stress-free. The pesto pasta salad is full of great herby flavours.

Serving Size: 4 people

Cooking Time: 15 mins

Ingredients:

- 1 cup of fusilli pasta (or pasta of your choice)
- 4 tablespoons of basil pesto
- 1 cup of broccoli (chopped)
- ½ cup of black olives (chopped)
- 1 cup of cherry tomatoes
- 1 cup of baby spinach
- Salt and pepper to taste

Method:

In a saucepan, add the pasta and broccoli and cover with water.

Boil the pasta and broccoli until tender.

Once the pasta and broccoli are cooked, remove from the heat. Then, add the olives, tomatoes and spinach and mix well.

Add salt, pepper and pesto. Mix together and set aside

Once the pasta is completely cool, divide it into 4 plastic cups and put in a cooler.

Melon and Strawberry Fruit Salad

Put a little twist on a boring fruit salad by making this vibrant sweet version. It is perfect for an afternoon picnic in late spring.

Serving Size: 4 people

Cooking Time: 10 mins

Ingredients:

- 1 cup of strawberries (chopped)
- 1 cup of watermelon (chopped)
- 1 cup of honeydew melon (chopped)
- 1 cup of red grapes (halved)
- ¼ cup of fresh mint leaves (chopped finely)

Method:

In a large bowl, add the chopped fruits and mint leaves and mix well until all the ingredients are well combined.

Divide into individual serving cups or containers and pack in a cooler.

Take to your picnic and enjoy.

Fancy Fruit and Cheese Cups

These fancy cups are perfect for a fancier picnic, whether it's a friend's celebration, a romantic picnic or even a kid's birthday. The simple trick of putting very simple ingredients in special cups will turn an ordinary picnic into a fancy affair.

Serving Size: 4 people

Cooking Time: 10 mins

Ingredients:

- 1 cup of strawberries (halved)
- 1 cup of red grapes
- 2 hard cheese slices such as cheddar, gouda, Swiss
- 4 salty pretzel biscuits
- 4 prosciutto ham slices or deli meat of your choice

Method:

In a cup of your choice, place the grapes.

Add the pretzel biscuits towards the back and place the cheese slices in front of the biscuits.

Add the strawberries and ham slices.

Virgin Mimosa

If you want to make your picnic a fancy affair, this drink is what you are looking for. It is non-alcoholic, so it is family-friendly and something that kids and adults can enjoy together.

Serving Size: 4 people

Cooking Time: 5 mins

Ingredients:

- 2 cups of fresh orange juice
- 2 cups of bitter lemon soda

Method:

In plastic champagne glasses, fill with the orange juice halfway.

Top the orange juice with the bitter lemon soda.

Repeat 3 times and serve.

Turkey Croissant Sandwiches

These sandwiches are easy to make and will make everyone happy. Using a croissant helps add a buttery flavour to the sandwiches making them no need for mayonnaise or butter.

Serving Size: 4 people

Cooking Time: 10 mins

Ingredients:

- 4 full butter croissants
- 4 large tomatoes (sliced)
- 8 turkey slices
- 4 cheddar cheese slices
- 4 washed and dried large romaine lettuce leaves
- Salt and pepper to taste

Method:

Cut the croissants in half and place the lettuce leaves on the bottom side.

Top with the tomato slices and season with salt and black pepper.

Top with the turkey slices and cheese slices.

Top with the other half of the croissants and wrap in foil.

Pack the sandwiches in a cooler and take them to the picnic.

Sweet Kebabs

One of the things that can ruin a picnic is getting ants in your food. Ants are usually attracted to sweet things. Putting sweets on kebab sticks helps to prevent this. It also makes more fun for everybody.

Serving Size: 4 people

Cooking Time: 5 mins

Ingredients:

- 2 cups of a selection of soft sweets made from gummies and marshmallows

Method:

Get 4 kebab sticks, then arrange and divide the sweets between the sticks.

Wrap with foil and pack in a cooler.

Caprese Salad in A Cup

Caprese salads are very popular because they combine the sweetness of plum tomatoes and the freshness of basil. Putting Caprese salad in a cup is good for serving at a picnic.

Serving Size: 4 people

Cooking Time: 15 mins

Ingredients:

- 2 cups of baby plum tomatoes (sliced in half)
- 1 medium full-fat mozzarella cheese ball (chopped into cubes)
- ¼ cup of fresh basil (chopped)
- Salt and pepper to taste

Method:

In a large bowl, add the tomatoes, mozzarella cheese and basil.

Add salt and pepper and mix well until everything is combined.

Divide the salad into 4 small plastic cups.

Cover and pack in a cooler until you are ready to serve.

Rainbow In a Cup

Fruit salads are a picnic favourite, but layering fruit salad like a rainbow and serving it in separate cups help to add an extra special touch.

Serving Size: 4 people

Cooking Time: 15 mins

Ingredients:

- 1 cup of grapes (chopped)
- ½ cup of strawberries (chopped)
- ½ cup of blueberries
- 1 cup of watermelon (chopped)

Method:

Make sure the fruits are chopped into evenly size.

Get 4 plastic cups and layer the fruits in the cups so that they are colour-coded.

Cover the cups and place them in a cooler until you are ready to serve

Cucumber Sandwiches

These sandwiches are very popular in England and are commonly associated with summer and the Wimbledon tennis tournament. This is a great recipe to make if you're planning a summertime picnic.

Serving Size: 4 people

Cooking Time: 15 mins

Ingredients:

- 8 white bread slices
- ½ large cucumber (cut into thin slices)
- ¼ cup of fresh dill (finely chopped)
- ½ cup of cream cheese
- Salt and pepper to taste

Method:

Cut the crust of the bread out.

In a small bowl, mix the cream cheese, dill, salt and pepper.

Spread the cream cheese mixture evenly over each bread slice.

On one bread slice, lay the cucumber slices evenly over and top with another bread slice (repeat this 3 times).

Cut the sandwiches into 4, then put them in an airtight container. Put in a cooler until you're ready to serve.

Easy Peasy Chocolate Cornflake Cups

This sweet snack is great for picnics because it is very easy to make and an easy crowd-pleaser.

Serving Size: 4 people

Cooking Time: 15 mins

Ingredients:

- 4 cups of cornflakes
- 500g of milk chocolate

Method:

In a small bowl, melt the chocolate by heating it in the microwave in 30-second intervals. Every 30 seconds, remove the bowl and stir the chocolate all together. Do this until the chocolate is fully melted with no hard parts.

In a large bowl, add the cornflakes and melted chocolate and stir until well mixed.

On a tray, lay 12 cupcake cases out and spoon 2 heaped tablespoons of the mixture in each cupcake case.

Put the tray in the fridge for a minimum of 2 hours until the chocolate is firmly set.

When you are ready for your picnic, pack the cups in an airtight container and put them in a cooler.

Rice Krispies Squares

This snack is easy to make and great for picnics in any season, and it's an easy recipe for kids to help with.

Serving Size: 4 people

Cooking Time: 15 mins

Ingredients:

- 4 cups of Rice Krispies cereal
- 2 cups of marshmallows

Method:

In a small bowl, add the marshmallows and heat in the microwave in 30-second intervals. Every 30 seconds, remove the bowl and stir the marshmallows all together. Do this until the marshmallows are fully melted with no hard parts.

In a large bowl, add the cereal and marshmallows and stir until well mixed.

Line a rectangular baking tray or dish with baking paper/parchment paper.

Place the mixture in the dish and put in the fridge for a minimum of 2 hours until it is firmly set.

Once it is firmly set, remove it from the dish and cut into 12 even squares.

Savory Snack Box

When going for a picnic, packing the snacks in individual boxes makes things much easier and cleaner.

Serving Size: 4 people

Cooking Time: 15 mins

Ingredients:

- 20 savoury cheese crackers
- 20 of cheddar cheese slices
- 20 of large salami slices or deli meat of your choice
- 2 cups of walnuts
- 2 cups of dried apricots (dried fruit of your choice e.g., figs and dates)

Method:

Evenly divide the ingredient into 4 airtight containers.

Cover and place in a cooler until you are ready to serve.

Fruit Snack Box

This is a fruit and dip snack box that is easy to make and easy to clean up.

Serving Size: 4 people

Cooking Time: 15 mins

Ingredients:

- 2 cups of smooth peanut butter
- 2 apples (sliced evenly)
- 1 medium cucumber (cut into long sticks)
- 2 large cucumbers (cut into long sticks)
- 2 cups of grapes

Method:

Divide the peanut butter into 4 small containers.

Evenly divide the ingredients into 4 airtight containers.

Cover and place in a cooler until you are ready to serve.

Salted Caramel Popcorn

Popcorn is loved by many, and salted caramel is a very popular flavour. This recipe will add a sweet and salty surprise to your picnic.

N.B: If the recipe is too sweet, you can reduce the sugar.

Serving Size: 4 people

Cooking Time: 30 mins

Ingredients:

- 2 cups of corn kernels
- ¼ cup of vegetable oil
- 2 tablespoons of salt
- ½ cup of butter
- ¼ cup of double cream
- ½ cup of brown sugar

Method:

In a large saucepan, add the oil, then add the corn kernels making sure that they are evenly placed around the saucepan.

Cover the pan and put it on medium heat until the kernels have popped.

Put the popcorn in a large bowl and set aside.

In another saucepan, add the butter and sugar until they are fully melted together.

Add the double cream and stir until well combined.

Take off the heat and add the salt.

Add the caramel to the popcorn making sure to mix well.

Put the popcorn on a baking sheet and bake in the oven at 180°C for 15 minutes.

Remove from the oven and set aside until cool.

When fully cooled, put the popcorn in an airtight container until you are ready to serve.

Cheesy Popcorn

This recipe adds some great savoury flavour to a popular snack.

Serving Size: 4 people

Cooking Time: 30 mins

Ingredients:

- 2 cups of corn kernels
- 2 tablespoons of vegetable oil
- 1 tablespoon of mixed herbs
- 1 teaspoon of garlic powder
- 1 teaspoon of onion powder
- 1 teaspoon of salt
- 1 teaspoon of pepper
- ¼ cup of parmesan cheese (grated)

Method:

In a large saucepan, add the oil, then add the corn kernels making sure that they are evenly placed around the saucepan.

Cover the pan and put it on medium heat until the kernels have popped.

Put the popcorn in a large bowl and set aside.

In a bowl, add the cheese, salt, pepper, garlic powder, onion powder and mixed herbs.

Add the cheese mixture to the popcorn and mix very well.

Add the popcorn to an airtight container.

Avocado and Chickpea Sandwiches

These sandwiches are great for a picnic because they use avocado. The avocado will add a creamy flavour to them without making the bread soggy. The chickpeas also add a lot of proteins, so the sandwiches will keep you feeling full.

Serving Size: 4 people

Cooking Time: 15 mins

Ingredients:

- 8 brown bread slices
- 1 large avocado
- ½ cup of chickpeas
- Salt and pepper to taste
- 2 large tomatoes (sliced)
- 1 medium romaine lettuce
- ¼ cup of basil pesto

Method:

In a large bowl, add the chickpeas and avocado flesh.

Mash the chickpeas and avocado flesh together until a well-mixed mash is formed (using the back of a fork can help with this).

Add salt and pepper, mix well and set aside.

On a tray, lay 4 bread slices out and cover them with the pesto.

Lay the romaine lettuce leaves and tomato slices.

Spread some avocado and chickpea mash.

Cover with some more lettuce leaves and the other bread slices.

Wrap the sandwiches in foil and put them in a cooler.

N.B: these sandwiches can also be grilled.

Snack Box

By pre-dividing the snacks, you will make sure that everyone gets a fair share of food at your picnic. This box will stop kids from fighting over things and make cleaning up very easy.

Serving Size: 4 people

Cooking Time: 10 mins

Ingredients:

- 4 sandwiches of your choice
- 4 packets of crisps
- 4 bottles water/juice
- 4 apples

Method:

Divide the ingredients into 4 airtight containers.

Put your containers in a cooler and make your way to your picnic.

N.B: you could label your containers or have each of them in a different colour.

Spinach and Mushroom Frittata

This recipe is tasty and can be eaten warm or cold. It has lots of filling ingredients, and it's easy to make.

Serving Size: 4 people

Cooking Time: 30 mins

Ingredients:

- 6 eggs
- 1 cup of broccoli (chopped)
- 2 cups of baby spinach
- 1 cup of mushrooms (chopped)
- ½ large onion
- 1 tablespoon of mixed herbs
- 2 tablespoons of vegetable oil
- Salt and pepper to taste

Method:

Preheat the oven to 180°C.

In a medium-sized frying pan, heat the oil and add the onion.

When the onion has become soft, add the broccoli and mushrooms.

In a small bowl, beat the eggs and mix the herbs, salt and pepper, then whisk all together.

Once the broccoli has softened, add the egg mixture.

Evenly spread the baby spinach over the eggs and mix.

Remove the pan from the heat and place in the oven for 10 minutes.

Remove from the oven and allow to cool.

Once cooled, divide the frittata into 8 equal slices and place in an airtight container.

Butter Herb Corn

Not only is sweetcorn very tasty, but it's also full of great vitamins and minerals that make it very healthy. The corn is high in vitamin B6, potassium, folate etc., making it one of nature's sweetest medicines.

This recipe can be enjoyed warm or cold, and it's great finger food for picnics.

Serving Size: 4 people

Cooking Time: 20 mins

Ingredients:

- 4 large sweetcorn
- 4 tablespoons of salted butter
- 1 tablespoon of mixed herbs

Method:

Preheat the oven to 180°C.

In a small bowl, mix the butter and herbs together.

Using your hands, spread the butter mixture over the corn making sure each one is evenly coated.

Wrap the corn in foil and bake in the oven for 15 minutes.

Remove the corn from the oven, but do not unwrap it from the foil until you are ready to eat.

Lemon Coconut Squares

This easy bake is zesty and sweet. It's perfect for a summer picnic because it's light and fluffy and smells amazing.

Serving Size: 4 people

Cooking Time: 30 mins

Ingredients:

- 200g of butter
- 200g of sugar
- 200g of flour
- 200ml of milk
- 4 large eggs
- 1 teaspoon of vanilla essence
- Pinch of salt
- The zest of 3 lemons
- The juice of 2 large lemons
- 4 tablespoons of desiccated coconut

Method:

Preheat the oven to 180°C.

In a large bowl, add the butter, milk, vanilla essence, sugar, lemon zest, lemon juice and salt and whisk together until light and fluffy.

Add the eggs to the mixture one at a time. Each egg should be well mixed before adding the next.

Add the flour and coconut and gently fold making sure to not over mix.

Pour the mixture into a rectangle baking dish and bake in the oven for 25 minutes.

Remove from the oven. Allow to cool completely, then divide into 12 even squares.

Peanut Butter and Jelly Sandwiches

These sandwiches are famous around the world because they are so delicious. The savoury peanut butter and sweet jam make a wonderful combination that is loved by adults and kids alike. Using chunky peanut butter adds some crunch. Make sure to use the best quality jam and peanut butter because they will make all the difference.

Serving Size: 4 people

Cooking Time: 10 mins

Ingredients:

- 8 salty white bread slices
- ½ cup of strawberry jam
- ½ cup of chunky peanut butter

Method:

On a tray, lay the bread slices out.

On half of them, generously spread the peanut butter and spread jam for the other.

Combine each jam spread bread slice with one peanut butter spread bread slice, then cut in half

Place the sandwiches in an airtight container until you are ready to serve.

Turkey Sandwiches

These turkey sandwiches are great for picnics because they are a crowd-pleaser. Even picky eaters will enjoy their simple flavour.

Serving Size: 4 people

Cooking Time: 10 mins

Ingredients:

- 8 bread slices
- 1 cup of mayonnaise
- ¼ cup of fresh coriander (finely chopped)
- ½ teaspoon of salt
- ½ teaspoon of black pepper
- 8 turkey slices

Method:

In a small bowl, mix the mayonnaise, coriander, salt and pepper.

On a tray, lay all the bread out and spread the mayonnaise mixture on each bread slice.

On one bread slice, add one turkey slice and cover with another bread slice.

Cut the bread into finger size and place in an airtight container.

Sandwich and Fruit Kebab

This recipe is a great way to add some fun to your picnic. It's very simple but will add a special touch to your day.

Serving Size: 4 people

Cooking Time: 10 mins

Ingredients:

- 1 peanut butter and jam sandwich
- 1 turkey sandwich
- 1 cup of grapes
- ½ large cucumber (cut into slices)
- 1 cup of strawberries (cut in half)

Method:

Cut the sandwiches into 9 even squares.

On a kebab stick, arrange the ingredients in order of one sandwich, one strawberry, one cucumber, one grape, one sandwich, one strawberry, one cucumber, one grape and one sandwich.

Repeat this 7 times until all the ingredients have been used.

Cover with foil and place in a cooler.

Tuna and Avocado Wrap

This tuna wrap is packed with high complex carbohydrates and proteins that will help fill you up on your picnic. Using a tortilla wrap helps to stop the filling from making a mess.

Serving Size: 4 people

Cooking Time: 20 mins

Ingredients:

- 4 wholemeal tortillas
- 1 can of tuna
- ½ cup of mayonnaise
- 1 large avocado (sliced)
- 1 cup of baby spinach

Method:

In a bowl, add the tuna and mayonnaise, mix well and set aside

Lay one tortilla on a plate and spread a quarter of the tuna mixture evenly over the tortilla.

Top it with the baby spinach leaves

Add a quarter of the avocado and wrap the tortilla, then cut in half and place in an airtight container

Easy Picnic Brownies

These brownies are rich and chocolatey and have delicious chunks of Snickers throughout. They are easy to make so that it means they cut down on picnic preparation.

Serving Size: 4-6 people

Cooking Time: 40 mins

Ingredients:

- 1 cup of oil
- 4 eggs
- ½ cup of cocoa powder
- ½ cup of chocolate (melted)
- 1 cup of flour
- 1 ½ cups of sugar
- Pinch of salt
- 1 teaspoon of vanilla essence
- 3 Snickers bars (chopped)

Method:

Preheat the oven to 180°C.

In a large bowl, add the oil and sugar and mix well.

Add the eggs, salt and vanilla essence.

Add the melted chocolate and mix well.

Add the cocoa powder and flour and fold in gently.

Add the Snickers chunks and fold in well.

Line a square baking dish with baking paper.

Pour the brownie mixture into the baking dish and bake for 25 minutes.

Remove the brownie and allow it to cool, then cut it into 12 even squares and pack in an airtight container.

Banana and Peanut Butter Rice Cakes

These rice cakes are gluten-free and low calorie. They are a great snack if you are having a picnic with anyone on a special diet.

Serving Size: 4 people

Cooking Time: 10 mins

Ingredients:

- 4 rice cakes
- 4 tablespoons of crunchy peanut butter
- 2 large bananas (cut into slices)
- 2 teaspoons of ground cinnamon

Method:

Lay the rice cakes out on a plate.

Spread over the peanut butter on each rice cake.

Cover the peanut butter with the banana slices.

Sprinkle the cinnamon over each rice cake.

Conclusion

The recipes in this cookbook are kept simple on purpose. The goal of this is to inspire you to be creative and fun in the kitchen. For example, add extra seasoning to *Cheesy Popcorn* and add chocolate chips to *Banana and Peanut Butter Rice Cakes*. Use the recipes as the inspiration for you to make your very own wonderful recipes.

The most important thing about having a picnic is spending quality time with your family and friends. That quality time doesn't have to begin at the picnic; it can begin in the preparation. You can make the recipes with your family and friends. You can make a game where you assign one recipe to each guest of your picnic and then judge who made the best dish. You can involve your family and friends from the very beginning of planning the picnic to the end of enjoying the picnic.

In conclusion, we hope this cookbook inspires you to have fun with your loved ones at picnics.

About the Author

Since he was a child, Logan King enjoyed watching his mom cook. For him, it was even more fun than playing with his friends. That's how he fell in love with cooking. In fact, the first thing he ever cooked on his own was a cupcake, a surprise for his little sister, which not even his mom was expecting.

Now, supported by the whole family he is constantly sharing new recipes of his own creations. He finished a gastronomy academy when he was 18 and continued his career as a chef and recipe developer.

Now his goal is to educate and help people fell in love with cooking as he did. Actually, he is advising mothers and fathers to give their children an opportunity in the kitchen, because they never know, maybe their kid could be the next top chef.

Even though he pursued a career as a chef, his cookbooks are designed for everyone, with and without cooking experience. He even says, "even if you don't know where your knife is you will be able to do my recipes."

The gastronomy field is large and there is no end in the options, ingredient combinations, and cooking techniques. That's why he tries his best to keep his audience informed about the newest recipes, and even give them a chance to modify his recipes so that they can find a new one, one that they can call their own.

Appendices

I am not stopping with this book. There are going to a lot more so make sure you are ready for the amazing recipes that you will be able to get from me. You can always be sure that they are going to be simple and easy to follow.

But thank you for choosing my book. I know that you haven't made a mistake and you will realize that too, well, as soon as you start making the recipes.

Please do share your experience about the written as well as the practical part of this book. Leave feedback that will help me and other people, I'll greatly apricate this.

Thank you once more

Have a great adventure with my book

Yours Truly

Logan King

Printed in Great Britain
by Amazon